MARTIN LUTHER KING, JR.

Anita Ganeri
and Nicola Barber

Raintree

Chicago, Illinois

© 2003 Raintree
Published by Raintree, a division of
Reed Elsevier Inc., Chicago, Illinois

Library of Congress Cataloging-in-Publication Data:

Ganeri, Anita, 1961-
  Martin Luther King, Jr. / Anita Ganeri and
Nicola Barber.
      p. cm.-- (20th Century History Makers)
Summary: A comprehensive biography of
civil rights leader Martin Luther
King, Jr., which points out how effectively
he used nonviolence as a weapon against
hatred and injustice. Includes
bibliographical references and index.
  ISBN 0-7398-5257-4 (HC)
  1. King, Martin Luther, Jr., 1929-1968--
Juvenile literature. 2. African Americans--
Biography--Juvenile literature. 3. Civil
rightsworkers--United States--Biography--
Juvenile literature. 4. Baptists--United
States--Clergy--Biography--Juvenile
literature. 5. African Americans--Civil
rights--History--20th century--Juvenile
literature. [1. King, Martin Luther, Jr.,
1929-1968. 2. Civil rights workers. 3.
Clergy. 4. Civil rights movements--History.
5. AfricanAmericans--Biography.] I. Barber,
Nicola. II. Title.
  E185.97.K5G356 2003
  323'.092--dc21
2003005774

Printed in Hong Kong/China. Bound in
the United States.

Picture credits
Front and back cover images:
Popperfoto

Corbis: pp 7, 10, 20-21, 23, 28, 32,
37, 41, 53, 81, 82-83
Hulton Archive: p 85
Magnum Photos: p 31(Dan Wiener)
Popperfoto: pp 2, 3, 5, 8, 25, 35, 43,
56, 59, 60-61, 71, 73, 74, 79, 87, 93,
98, 101, 103 (Tami Chappell/Reuters)
Topham: pp 12(AP), 15, 17, 19, 27,
38(Keystone), 45(AP), 46(AP), 48-49,
51(AP), 55(AP), 63(AP), 64-65, 66, 69,
77(AP), 89, 91, 95, 97

Text credit
"I Have a Dream" (text of speech,
pages 62–67) Reprinted by
arrangement with the Estate of Martin
Luther King Jr., c/o Writers House as
agent for the proprietor, New York,
N.Y.

Copyright 1963 Dr. Martin Luther
King Jr., copyright renewed 1991
Coretta Scott King

Martin Luther
King, Jr.
1929–1968

Contents

Introduction

Martin Luther King, Jr. (1929-1968), an African-American minister, was the greatest leader of the civil rights movement of the 1950s and 1960s.

Dr. King's powerful speeches won the support of millions and helped to ensure equal rights under the law for all.

On the evening of April 4, 1968, as he stood on the balcony of his motel in Memphis, Tennessee, Martin Luther King, Jr. was shot dead. King's murder shocked the globe. He was only 39, yet he had become one of the most influential civil rights leaders in the world.

King was born in Atlanta, Georgia, where he went to school and attended Ebenezer Baptist Church. His father and grandfather, and later King himself, served as ministers there. Throughout his life, his Christian faith was a strong support to him. King was a brilliant student, graduating at the top of his class and going on to earn a doctorate in theology from Boston University. This is where he met his wife-to-be, Coretta Scott. They were married in 1953 and had four children.

At that time in the United States, the issue of equal rights for everyone was a national concern. In the southern states, black people were treated like second-class citizens, and strict segregation laws were used to separate black and white people. King's experience of racial discrimination started at an early age. In 1955 King was asked to lead a boycott of the city buses in Montgomery, Alabama. A black passenger, Rosa Parks, had been arrested for refusing to give up her seat to a white passenger. This was the start of King's involvement in the civil rights movement. He struggled to bring about equal rights for all Americans.

In his most famous speech, given in Washington in 1963, King stated:

"I have a dream that my four little children will one day live in a nation where they will not be judged by the color of their skin but by the content of their character."

This book is the story of Martin Luther King, Jr. and his dream.

▶ *Martin Luther King, Jr. This photograph was taken in November 1961, when King was 32 years old.*

Early Life

Martin Luther King, Jr. was born in Atlanta, Georgia on January 15, 1929. He was the second child and first son of Alberta Williams King and Martin Luther King, Sr.

At his birth Martin was given the name Michael, after the name by which his father was commonly known. But when the boy was five, his father officially changed both their names to Martin, although Martin's family usually called him "ML." Young Martin was a healthy baby. He grew up in a loving home with his older sister, Willie Christine, and younger brother, Alfred Daniel.

Martin Luther King, Sr.

Martin Luther King, Sr. was pastor of the Ebenezer Baptist Church in Atlanta, Georgia. He and his family lived in a two-story house close to the church in a mostly black, fairly prosperous neighborhood. However, Reverend (Rev.) King had not always lived in such comfortable surroundings, and he knew what it was to be poor. His own father had worked as a farmer on a plantation in Georgia and his mother as a housecleaner for a white family. As a child he had experienced the vast differences between the ways white and black people lived.

When he was eighteen, King decided to leave the farm and go to Atlanta to get an education. He found daytime work and went to night classes to study for a high school diploma. He also became a minister in the Baptist church. In the early 1920s, he met Alberta Williams, daughter of the pastor of Ebenezer Baptist Church. The two were married in 1926. Rev. King became pastor of Ebenezer Baptist Church after the death of his father-in-law in 1931.

Growing up

The Christian faith was a major part of everyday life in the King household, and young Martin came to regard his church as a kind of second home. However, as he grew up, Martin

▲ The house at 501 Auburn Avenue, Atlanta, where Martin Luther King, Jr. was born in 1929.

The house is situated near Ebenezer Baptist Church, where King's father was pastor.

▲ Martin Luther King's father, Martin Sr., was a powerful speaker. This photograph shows him delivering a sermon in July 1975, before retiring at the end of his 44-year ministry.

gradually became aware of another part of everyday life in Atlanta—the segregation of black and white people. As a small child, Martin played with a white friend whose father owned a store near the King family house. One day, the friend's parents told their son that he was not allowed to play with Martin any longer. The reason they gave was that he was white and Martin was black.

This was Martin's first experience with segregation, and that evening he questioned his parents about it. For the first time, they explained about the system of segregation by race in the southern states and about the suffering and hardship it caused the African-American population.

Segregation in action

The segregation laws in Atlanta were strict. There were separate schools, theaters, and restaurants for black and white people. African-American children were not allowed to play in public parks. On the buses, white people traveled at the front, black people at the back. All these laws were made by white people to make the black population feel inferior. But Martin's parents told their son: "You are as good as anyone." Rev. King hated the so-called Jim Crow laws (see below) and refused to accept the system.

One day Rev. King took young Martin to buy shoes. A white shop assistant asked them to move to seats at the back of the shop. When Rev. King replied that they were quite happy

Jim Crow

The nickname given to the system of segregation by race in the United States was "Jim Crow." This name came from a song, *Jump, Jim Crow*. It formed part of the act of a white entertainer called Thomas Rice, who wore black make-up to perform the song. There was discrimination against black people throughout the United States after the abolition of slavery. In the north, there were no state laws segregating black and white, but in the South the situation was very different. There, states passed laws to segregate black and white people in all areas of life. There were even separate drinking fountains for "white" and "colored" people. The Jim Crow laws were meant to make black people feel like inferior, second-class citizens.

Ebenezer Baptist Church, shown in a 1968 photograph.

where they were, the salesperson became insistent. Rev. King refused to budge, saying that they would buy shoes where they were sitting or not at all. Then he took Martin's hand and left.

In addition to the Jim Crow laws, whites were often rude and insulting to blacks. In particular they called black men and women "boy" and "girl," even when speaking to adults.

Rev. King experienced this patronizing attitude on many

occasions, but he didn't take it lying down. On one occasion a traffic policeman pulled him over for a minor offense and said: "Let me see your driver's licence, boy." Rev. King retorted angrily, pointing to Martin: "That's a boy. I'm a man." When he refused to do as the officer asked unless he was addressed properly, the stunned policeman simply wrote out a ticket and moved on quickly.

These and other incidents of racial injustice made a powerful impression on the young Martin.

School days

Martin was a clever student, and he excelled in school. He was so bright, in fact, that he skipped a couple of grades in school. At the age of thirteen, he went to high school on the other side of Atlanta from his home.

When he traveled on the city's buses, he was forced by the Jim Crow laws to sit or stand at the back. Even if the back of the bus was full, black people were not permitted to sit on "whites-only" seats. And if the "white-only" section became full, black

From slavery to segregation

From 1861 to 1865, the United States was split by a horrific civil war between the northern (Union) and southern (Confederate) states. The main issue that sparked the fighting was slavery.

Since the 1500s black people had been brought by force from Africa to work as slaves in the Americas. But by the beginning of the 1800s, many people in the northern United States thought that slavery should be abolished in their country. However, in the South, white plantation owners relied on black slave labor and wished to preserve the old system. After four years of bitter fighting, the Union forces claimed victory.

Slavery was finally abolished in the United States in 1865, with the passing of the 13th amendment to the U.S. Constitution. However, discrimination against African Americans continued; segregation remained a fact of life throughout much of the South.

passengers were obliged to give up their seats to white passengers.

When he was fourteen, Martin was chosen to compete in an oratorical (public speaking) contest that was to

be held in Dublin, Georgia. He traveled to Dublin with one of his teachers and won the contest with his speech on "The Negro and the Constitution." On the journey back to Atlanta, the bus became full. When some white passengers boarded the bus, the driver ordered Martin and his teacher to give up their seats. At first, Martin refused, but his teacher urged him to obey the law. Martin stood in the aisle all the way back to Atlanta, but afterwards he said the incident made him "the angriest I have ever been in my life."

Morehouse College

At the age of fifteen, Martin went to Morehouse College in Atlanta to study sociology. He worked on a tobacco farm in Connecticut the summer before he started at Morehouse. It was the first time he had been away from home and the first time he had traveled to the northern states.

◀ *Segregation laws were rigidly enforced in Georgia. This 1961 photo shows a policeman about to force black customers to leave a whites-only restaurant lunch counter at an Atlanta bus terminal.*

Martin wrote his father that once they had passed Washington, there was no discrimination. "The white people here are very nice," he added. It lifted Martin's spirits to be able to go any place and sit anywhere he chose. It was bitterly hard to return to the South, and to segregation, at the end of the summer.

During other summer vacations, Martin took jobs as a manual laborer in Atlanta, working alongside whites and blacks. He experienced racism, but he also realized that social injustice applied to both poor white and poor black people.

In college he was encouraged to discuss the race problem and ways of working toward racial justice. He joined the Atlanta Intercollegiate Council and came to know more white people on equal terms. At the same time, Martin realized that he wanted to follow in his father's footsteps and enter the Baptist ministry. He gave a trial sermon in his father's church; it was a huge success. The following year, 1948, he was ordained assistant pastor at Ebenezer Baptist Church at the age of eighteen.

Marriage and Ministry

In September 1948 Martin Luther King, Jr. started studying for a Bachelor of Arts degree in divinity at Crozer Theological Seminary in Chester, Pennsylvania.

Although King had graduated from Morehouse College in the spring of 1948, he was determined to continue his studies. Crozer was one of the best religious colleges in the country. It was also in Pennsylvania, a northern state well away from the restrictive segregation laws of the south. However, King was one of only 6 black students out of the 100 students attending the college.

Despite enjoying the independence and freedom of his new life away from Atlanta, King was very aware of the impression he was making on his mostly white fellow peers. He tried hard to avoid being identified with the white racist's stereotypical view of a African Americans. King became very self-conscious and later wrote that he was "grimly serious for a time…."

King worked very hard at Crozer and got A grades for every course that he took. He read widely, particularly the works of the world's greatest philosophers. It was when reading an essay by the American philosopher and writer, Henry David Thoreau (1817–1862), that King first came across an idea that was to have a major influence on him throughout his life and work.

Civil disobedience

King first read Thoreau's essay *On Civil Disobedience* while he was attending Morehouse College. Written in 1849, this essay advanced the idea that first and foremost people should act according to their own personal sense of right and wrong:

▶ *King was greatly influenced by the work of philosopher and writer Henry David Thoreau. Especially important was Thoreau's belief that individuals should act according to their consciences.*

"Must the citizen ever for a moment, or in the least degree, resign his conscience to the legislator? Why has every man a conscience then? I think that we should be men first, and subjects afterward. It is not desirable to cultivate a respect for the law, so much as for the right. The only obligation that I have a right to assume is to do at any time what I think right."

Thoreau went on to argue that if someone believed a law to be unjust, he or she should follow his or her own moral sense and refuse to obey it. By such noncooperation with an evil system, even the voice of a single person could make a difference and change that law:

"Unjust laws exist: shall we be content to obey them, or shall we endeavor to amend them, and obey them until we have succeeded, or shall we transgress them at once? Men, generally, under such a government as this, think that they ought to wait until they have persuaded the majority to alter them. They think that, if they should resist, the remedy would be worse than the evil. But it is the fault of the government itself that the remedy is worse than the evil. It makes it worse. Why is it not more apt to anticipate and provide for reform?"

Thoreau put his own theories into practice when he refused to pay his taxes. He did this to express his opposition to the extension of slavery into the new territories won by the United States after the end of its war with Mexico in 1848. As a result, he spent a night in prison. Thoreau's words about his experience would soon ring true for Martin Luther King Jr., as he started on his own lifetime's campaign: "Under a government that imprisons unjustly, the true place for a just man is also a prison."

Nonviolent resistance

For King the outstanding idea in Thoreau's essay was that unjust laws could be challenged by passive, nonviolent resistance. Through his reading, he began to try to understand how he could use this idea to change the lives of African Americans.

One day King attended a lecture about the Indian leader, Mahatma Gandhi. The lecturer spoke movingly about Gandhi's life and teachings, and King was fascinated. He immediately bought books about Gandhi.

▶ *Another great inspiration for Martin Luther King, Jr. was the philosophy of nonviolence preached by the Indian leader, Mahatma Gandhi (1869–1948).*

What appealed to King about Gandhi was that he had used the power of nonviolent protest to oppose British rule in India (see right). Gandhi's methods of civil disobedience included fasts, marches, actions such as lying down in the streets, strikes, and boycotting British goods. He called this campaign "war without violence," and it was ultimately successful. Gandhi's actions and teachings provided the inspiration for Martin Luther King, Jr. to begin his lifelong struggle against the evil of racial discrimination.

Love and marriage

King graduated from Crozer Theological Seminary in 1951. He was the top student in his class, and he won a grant to carry on his studies. He decided to go to Boston University to work for a doctorate at its School of Theology. His studies at Boston over the next three years only served to strengthen his conviction that nonviolent resistance was an extremely powerful weapon.

Martin's life at Boston was not all work, however. He dated girls and on many evenings could be found listening to jazz in the nightclubs of Boston.

Mahatma Gandhi (1869-1948)

One of the greatest leaders of the 20th century, Gandhi helped to free India from British colonial rule. He did so by resisting the British through a long campaign of nonviolent action. Gandhi called this method of peaceful protest *satyagraha*, meaning truth (*satya*) persistence (*graha*).

Gandhi believed passionately that the use of violence only encouraged more violence in return. His method of *satyagraha* took a great deal of courage, but it proved highly effective. Perhaps the most famous example of Gandhi's peaceful methods was the Salt March, undertaken in 1930. This was in protest against a British law that made it a crime to possess salt—an essential commodity—not bought from and taxed by the government.

Gandhi and hundreds of followers walked 229 miles (368 kilometers) to the Indian coast, where they broke the law by symbolically making salt from seawater. Gandhi, and many others, were imprisoned by the British authorities for this protest.

Then one day in 1952, he asked a friend, who was studying at the New England Conservatory of Music, if he knew any

▶ *A photograph of Gandhi leading the Salt March in 1930 as a protest against British rule over India. He eventually forced change through peaceful means.*

nice, attractive young ladies. His friend gave him the phone number of a fellow music student, and so it was that Martin met Coretta Scott.

On their first date, Martin and Coretta had lunch together. They found it easy to talk to each other, and it soon became apparent that they had many interests in common, including the question of racial injustice. At the end of the date, Martin told Coretta that she possessed all the qualities he had ever wanted in a wife: character, intelligence, personality, and beauty. Coretta was astounded.

After that, the two saw each other frequently, but Coretta did have some doubts. She was training at the conservatory to become a concert singer, and she knew that marriage to King would mean the end of these ambitions. Nevertheless, she accepted King's proposal and the two were married on June 18, 1953, in a ceremony conducted by King's father.

▶ *A view of Crozer Theological Seminary, where Martin Luther King, Jr. studied for his B.A. in divinity. Crozer was situated in Pennsylvania, well away from the harsh segregation laws of the South.*

Black and White

After their marriage, Martin and Coretta King returned to Boston to complete their studies.

Coretta received her degree at the New England Conservatory in June 1954, and King started to write the thesis that would earn him his doctorate in 1955. At the same time, he started to think about his future. Should he accept one of the academic posts that he had already been offered, or should he pursue a career as a minister in the church? The academic posts were tempting, but King felt a strong calling to continue his work as a pastor. Two churches in the North were interested in him, one in Massachusetts, and one in New York.

Then one day King received a letter from Dexter Avenue Baptist Church in Montgomery, Alabama. The church was looking for a pastor, and asked if he would give a trial sermon the next time he was in the South. King replied that he would be delighted to preach there the next time he was home.

A difficult decision

In January 1954 King went to Montgomery to preach to the congregation at Dexter. He was unusually nervous. He had preached many sermons in his time as a minister, but none to try to get a job. He told himself over and over again to keep God in the foreground and himself in the background and remember that he was "a channel of the gospel and not the source." Then, everything would be all right.

The sermon went well, and about a month later King was offered the job at Dexter. The time had come for some difficult decisions. Martin and Coretta talked and talked about what to do. They both felt happy in the North, away from the segregation and racism of the South. They discussed what it would be like to raise their future children in the South, with all the restrictions of segregation.

▲ *This photograph shows Dexter Avenue Baptist Church in Montgomery, Alabama. In 1954 Dr. King became a pastor here.*

Finally, however, they decided to make the move to Montgomery. The South was their home and they both felt that they could do something to improve conditions for African Americans. They also sensed that things were beginning to change in the South and they wanted to be there to be a part of any new developments. In April 1954 King accepted the offer from Dexter.

Montgomery

Montgomery is the capital of the southeastern state of Alabama. It is one of the oldest cities in the United States. At the start of the American Civil War in 1861, it became the capital of the Confederate states. For this reason it is often known as the "Cradle of the Confederacy." When the Kings moved to Montgomery in 1954, it was a strictly segregated city. The Kings had no choice but to live in the "blacks-only" section of town. There were roughly 90,000 white people and 50,000 black people in Montgomery, yet the two races lived almost entirely separate existences.

Much to King's dismay, most black people in the city seemed to accept this state of affairs. The white majority had made the black minority feel so inferior that, for most African Americans, challenging the way of life in Montgomery seemed completely out of the question.

There were, however, some notable exceptions. One of the areas where discontent was growing among the black population was on the city's buses. The buses provided the only means of transportation for a large percentage of black people in Montgomery. Yet all the bus drivers were white and most were rude and insulting to their black passengers. Black passengers had to pay at the front of the bus, but many drivers then made them come in through the back doors. Often, a driver would close the doors and move off after a black person had paid but before he or she had boarded.

In addition, under Montgomery's Jim Crow laws, segregation was strictly enforced on the buses. Just as in Martin's youth in Atlanta, black people could only sit at the back of the bus, and if the "whites-only" seats were full, a black person was obliged to give up his or her seat to a standing white person. What was more, if a white person sat down next to a black person, the black person was automatically expected to stand up. All of this caused huge resentment among black people.

▶ *This picture of the interior of a bus in Dallas, Texas in 1956, demonstrates how black passengers had to sit at the back; whites sat at the front.*

Mrs. Rosa Parks

In December 1955 a tailor's assistant named Rosa Parks got on a bus in the center of Montgomery. She was tired after a hard day in the department store where she worked. She took a seat in the "unreserved" section at the back of the bus. But the bus soon filled up, and when a white man got on the bus and could not find a seat, the bus driver ordered Mrs. Parks to give up her seat. She refused. The driver then threatened to call the police. Mrs. Parks was unmoved. She was duly arrested, taken to a police station, and charged with breaking the city's segregation laws.

In fact, three other people had been arrested for refusing to give up their seats on the buses in 1955. Now, many African-American leaders in Montgomery felt that the time had come for their community to pull together to challenge the situation on the buses. Mrs. Parks was a well-known member of the black community, and she had been secretary of the local branch of the National Association for the Advancement of Colored People (NAACP). The time had come for the black people of the city to rally in support of her action. Black leaders, including Martin Luther King Jr., called for a boycott of the buses and organized a meeting that same evening.

Dr. King offered the use of his church as a meeting place. He was amazed at the number of people who

The boycott

This was the message on the leaflet that was handed out to the black community of Montgomery:

"Don't ride the bus to work, to town, to school, or any place Monday, December 5. Another Negro woman has been arrested and put in jail because she refused to give up her bus seat. Don't ride the buses to work, to town, to school, or anywhere on Monday. If you work, take a cab, or share a ride, or walk. Come to a mass meeting, Monday at 7:00 p.m., at the Holt Street Baptist Church for further instruction."

▶ *Rosa Parks was arrested for refusing to give up her seat to a white passenger on a Montgomery bus. Here she is with her lawyer, Charles Langford, on February 24, 1956.*

turned up: more than 40 in all. They agreed that African Americans should boycott the buses for one day, on Monday, December 5. They issued a message to Montgomery's black population (see page 26) and decided to spread the word about the boycott at church services on Sunday.

In the King household, Sunday night was a tense time. Would the boycott work or not? Coretta had recently given birth to the Kings' first child, Yolanda Denise, and that night the baby would not settle. Eventually her weary parents went to sleep. The following morning, they were both up early. As luck would have it, there was a bus stop within sight of their house. They watched with trepidation as the first bus of the morning drove slowly past. It was empty. A few minutes later, another one passed, and it, too, was empty. A third passed with just two white passengers. Dr. and Mrs. King were jubilant. The boycott was working perfectly.

◀ *Black students jeer as an empty bus passes during the Montgomery boycott. Dr. King believed that by boycotting the buses, black people were withdrawing their cooperation from an evil system.*

The Montgomery Bus Boycott

The bus boycott by the black community of Montgomery on December 5, 1955 was an almost total success. The question was: What to do next?

At nine o'clock on the morning of the bus boycott, Dr. King drove to City Hall in Montgomery to watch the trial of Rosa Parks. She was found guilty of breaking the segregation laws and fined $14. That afternoon, King met with the other black community leaders who had organized the boycott, including Ralph Abernathy, minister of the First Baptist Church in Montgomery, and E.D. Nixon, president of the Montgomery branch of the NAACP. There was to be a mass meeting that evening (see page 26), so the leaders needed to come up with a plan.

They decided to form a new organization, which they named the Montgomery Improvement Association (MIA). In a matter of minutes, Martin Luther King, Jr. had been elected president of the MIA. He had only recently turned down the chance to be president of the local NAACP, in order to spend more time on his ministry. He wondered what Mrs. King would say.

The problem faced by the MIA was this: Would the boycott fizzle out if it was extended for another day? It was eventually decided to see what the mood at the meeting was like. If it was enthusiastic and the meeting was well attended, the boycott would continue. With less than an hour to prepare a speech to address the meeting, Dr. King went home to tell his wife about becoming president of the MIA. He was apprehensive about her reaction. King need not have worried, because Coretta assured him that she would support whatever decision he made.

▶ *An informal photograph of Dr. and Mrs. King with their first child, Yolanda, on the steps of Dexter Avenue Baptist Church on March 3, 1956. In the background is the Alabama State Capitol.*

The meeting

Over 4,000 people attended the mass meeting, and their enthusiasm was obvious. After a hymn, King got up to make his speech. He spoke without notes, describing what had happened to Rosa Parks and the situation on the buses. He called for action, but then he warned people that this action must not be violent, and that they must be governed by law and order. His words inspired the crowd, and, when he sat down after 16 minutes, everyone was cheering and clapping wildly.

After this, Ralph Abernathy read aloud the MIA's demands to the bus companies and city officials. The boycott would continue until drivers treated black people politely; passengers must be seated on a first-come, first-served basis; and black bus drivers must be employed on buses that carried mainly African-American passengers. He asked all those in favor of these demands to stand, and every person immediately stood. The boycott was to continue.

Ralph Abernathy was minister of the First Baptist Church in Montgomery. He was involved with the bus boycott from the beginning, and later became a key figure in the civil rights movement along with King.

The boycott continues

After the excitement of the meeting, King settled down to organize more practical matters. People needed transportation to get around the city, to work and other places. At first, the black taxi companies helped out by charging only a small amount, 10 cents, for a ride. But the city authorities quickly put a stop to this practice by enforcing a law that limited taxis to a minimum fare of 45 cents.

King and the other MIA leaders decided to organize a car pool. More than 300 volunteers immediately offered to give their time to drive people around the city. The MIA established pick-up and drop-off points, and soon the car pool was operating more efficiently than the bus service ever had.

The city authorities called a meeting to discuss the demands of the black community. Dr. King spoke for the MIA, but it was soon obvious that the bus companies were not prepared to back down. They would offer black people polite treatment, but that was all. It was not enough and the boycott continued.

The city authorities and the police began to get tough. They arrested car pool drivers on the least pretense, with the result that volunteers began to leave the car pool, afraid that they would lose their licenses. Then, in January 1956, Dr. King himself was arrested, supposedly for driving five miles an hour over the speed limit. He was taken to Montgomery City Jail, where he was fingerprinted and put into a filthy cell with petty criminals. For the first time in his life he was in prison. But he remembered the words of Thoreau and Gandhi: "The real road to happiness lies in going to jail and undergoing suffering and privations there in the interest of one's country and religion…."

News of Dr. King's arrest quickly spread, and soon there was a crowd of supporters outside the jail. While Ralph Abernathy was trying to find the money to bail King out, the police panicked and released their prisoner. Dr. King was greatly reassured by the crowd of well-wishers. Now he knew for certain that he did not stand alone.

Threats and bombs

Since the beginning of the boycott, the Kings received threatening letters and phone calls at their home. By the end of January, these calls numbered 30 to 40

The influence of Gandhi

Not long after the boycott began, a white woman named Juliette Morgan wrote to a Montgomery newspaper. She compared the bus boycott to Gandhi's nonviolent movement in India. Her words set Dr. King thinking, and he and the other MIA leaders began to talk more and more about Gandhi and nonviolence. The idea caught on and soon everyone was discussing Gandhi and his methods. Although there were some who disagreed with the MIA's approach, nonviolence played a vital part in the eventual success of the Montgomery bus boycott.

every day. Some came from members of the Ku Klux Klan (KKK), a white secret society whose aim was to oppose any advancement or equal rights for African Americans and other minorities. Not surprisingly, the letters and calls upset and scared both Dr. and Mrs. King. One day, a white friend warned Dr. King that his life was in danger. Dr. King was very frightened; for the first time he felt in serious danger. But at a mass meeting, he

▶ *The Ku Klux Klan (KKK) was a white secret society that opposed any kind of advancement for black people and other minorities. This 1960s photo shows Klansmen picketing a desegregated hotel.*

tried to give an impression of strength, telling his supporters that no matter what happened to him, they should never respond with violence. He urged them to carry his message with the same dignity and restraint they had always shown.

On January 30, 1956, Dr. King went out in the evening to attend another mass meeting. As he was addressing the meeting, the news arrived that his house had been bombed. He dashed home. The bomb had exploded on the front porch. Luckily Mrs. King and Yolanda were in the back of the house and were unharmed.

A crowd of angry African Americans surged around the front of the house, furious at this attack on one of their leaders. Many of them were armed. White policemen were trying to clear the street, and the situation was rapidly getting out of control. Martin stepped out on to the porch and with a wave of his hand, asked for silence. He told the crowd not to panic, to put their faith in law and order because what they were doing was right. Once again he denounced violence and reiterated

plainly and forcefully: "If I am stopped this movement will not stop."

Desperate measures

By now, the city authorities were looking for any legal means to end the boycott. They found an old law against boycotts, and on the strength of this they started to round up and arrest all of the MIA leaders and all of the car pool drivers. Dr. King was away when these mass arrests started, but he hurried back to Montgomery. When he arrived at the city jail, he found an almost "holiday atmosphere." People were proudly giving themselves up for arrest. Once again, King was arrested.

The trial date was set for March 19. At his trial, Dr. King was found guilty of breaking the law against boycotts, and was released on bail. This time his trial and conviction made front-page news all over the world. Soon afterward, the MIA decided to take the whole matter to a higher court. They went to a Federal Court to ask the judges to end bus segregation in Alabama. The judges

A photograph of Martin Luther King, Jr. with Coretta taken at his court appearance on March 19, 1956.

ruled in favor of the MIA, but the city authorities stalled by taking the case to the Supreme Court. Meanwhile, the boycott continued.

While they were waiting for the Supreme Court ruling, the city authorities tried to shut down the car pool completely. Dr. King was in despair. He felt that the black people of Montgomery had suffered for long enough; now he was asking for more sacrifices. But on November 13, 1956, even as the case against the car pool was being heard, a decision came from the Supreme Court. The MIA had won. Bus segregation in Alabama had been ruled unlawful. The boycott had been an overwhelming success.

The order to end bus segregation arrived in Montgomery on December 20, 1956. The next morning, Dr. King was joined by Ralph Abernathy, E.D. Nixon, and others to ride on the first integrated bus in Montgomery.

The bus driver recognized Dr. King as he boarded the bus and expressed pleasure at driving him. The bus boycott was truly at an end.

◀ A view of the U.S. Supreme Court building in Washington, D.C. In November 1956 the court ruled that bus segregation was illegal.

Sit-ins and Freedom Rides

The victory in Montgomery was a landmark for African Americans. But the process of integration on the buses was not straightforward, and soon Montgomery plunged into a wave of violence.

Most white people in Montgomery accepted the bus integration. But a racist minority was determined to make trouble. Some of these people were armed and they shot at buses, especially at night. Then, on January 9, 1957, the home and church of Ralph Abernathy were both bombed. At the end of January, another bomb was thrown at the Kings' house, but luckily it did not explode.

These episodes deeply depressed Dr. King, and he began to feel personally responsible for the trouble and anxiety they caused. At a mass meeting, his emotions spilled over. He told the people that he prayed no one would die in the struggle for freedom in Montgomery. "If anyone has to die, let it be me, "he pleaded, to which the crowd shouted "No! No!" in reply.

Dr. King received many messages of support after this meeting, and he felt comforted. The black community was still strong in Montgomery and, unexpectedly, the city authorities arrested seven white men for the bombings. None were convicted, but the violence stopped, and bus integration continued more smoothly.

The SCLC

The events of the bus boycott changed many lives but none more so than that of Martin Luther King, Jr. He had emerged as a highly respected leader, and his fame now spread beyond Montgomery and across the nation.

This fame bothered Dr. King. He was deeply worried that he had achieved fame too soon and people would expect him to work miracles for the

Ralph Abernathy surveys the ruins of a church bombed by white extremists.

rest of his life. He doubted that he would be able to live up to expectations and people would say he had failed. He was offered many jobs but he decided to stay in Montgomery. However, he did become involved in the fight for civil rights across the South. He was elected president of a new organization, the Southern Leaders Conference, later called the Southern Christian Leadership Conference (SCLC). The aim of this organization was to coordinate African-American protest groups in nonviolent resistance throughout the South.

41

Despite the fact that every American citizen had the right to vote, in practice many African Americans in the South were denied that right. In order to vote, it was necessary to register, but many southern states made it very difficult for poor black people to do so. Often there were literacy tests, which were too difficult for anyone to pass. In many places, voters had to pay a special tax, which many poor black people simply could not afford.

As a result, the SCLC began a campaign it called the "Crusade for Citizenship." It aimed to gather evidence about abuses of voting rights in the South to inform the wider public that these abuses existed. It was also a crusade to persuade more black people to register to vote and to exercise their rights at the ballot box.

In 1957 King gave a speech at the "Prayer Pilgrimage for Freedom," held at the Lincoln Memorial in Washington, D.C. In front of thousands of people, he called for voting rights for African Americans. King appealed directly to the president to give African Americans the ballot, saying that if this were granted, the legislative halls of the nation could be filled with men of goodwill.

Trip to Ghana

In March 1957 the Kings traveled to the African continent. After years of struggle against the British, Ghana had finally won independence under the leadership of its first prime minister, Kwame Nkrumah. Dr. King was deeply moved by the independence ceremony and the cries of "Freedom, freedom" that he heard all around him. The Kings traveled back through Nigeria, still then a British colony, and then to Rome, Paris, Geneva, and London. King always remembered his visit to Ghana as one of the most vivid experiences of his life.

A brush with death

The "Crusade for Citizenship" started in 1958, and Dr. King worked tirelessly, traveling the length and breadth of the United States to give speeches. Somehow he also found time to write a book about the Montgomery bus boycott, titled *Stride Toward Freedom*. One day in 1958, he was in a department store in New York to sign copies of his book. A well-dressed black woman walked up to him and asked:

"Are you Martin Luther King Jr.?"

"Yes," Dr. King replied.

The next moment he felt something in his chest. He had been stabbed with a sharp letter opener. King was taken to Harlem Hospital, where he lay for many hours while the doctors prepared for the delicate and dangerous operation to remove the letter opener from his heart. The operation was a success. Afterward, the surgeon told him that if he had sneezed during those hours of waiting, the tip of the letter opener would have ruptured his heart, and it was likely he would have died.

After recovering from this attack, King decided to go to India. He had long wanted to visit the home of Gandhi before he plunged back once more into the hectic schedule of the SCLC. He and Coretta traveled with

▼ *The Kings traveled to India after Dr. King had recovered from a 1958 assassination attempt. Here they are pictured with the Prime Minister of India, Dr. Nehru.*

"I'm so happy that you didn't sneeze"

Of the hundreds of letters Dr. King received while he was recovering in the hospital, one seemed to him to have special significance. The message was a simple one, from a white female student who attended White Plains High School in White Plains, New York. She wrote that she had read about Dr. King's suffering in the newspaper and that he would have died if he'd so much as sneezed. "I'm simply writing to say that I'm so happy that you didn't sneeze."

a friend, and they were given an extremely warm reception from everyone they met.

Dr. King was deeply moved to visit the places where Gandhi worked and to meet his relatives. These events further convinced him that the most powerful weapon against oppression was resistance by nonviolent means.

Sit-ins

In 1959 Dr. King decided to leave Montgomery and move back to his hometown, Atlanta, and to his father's church, Ebenezer Baptist.

He was sad to leave Montgomery, but he knew that it would be easier to coordinate his work as a minister and as president of the SCLC in the larger, more important center of Atlanta.

The Kings' move to Atlanta coincided with a time when the civil rights movement in the South began to gain momentum. In February 1960 four black students in Greensboro, North Carolina, went to a store and sat at the "whites-only" counter. The assistant refused to serve them, but they sat at the counter until the store closed. Soon their example was being followed by students in other parts of the South. Many students wrote to Dr. King for advice, which he freely gave. He also traveled around the South to give encouragement and speeches to the protesting students.

As the sit-ins continued, the students were confronted with increasingly violent retaliation from the police, including beatings and

▶ *Montgomery Sheriff Mac Butler prepares to arrest a group of protesters (including Ralph Abernathy, third from left) staging a sit-in at a lunch counter.*

tear gas. But they continued undaunted and the sit-ins spread to other areas: swimming pools, libraries, theaters, hotels, or anywhere where there was racial segregation. As a result of the sit-ins, the segregation laws were eventually changed in many places.

Freedom Rides

Another famous nonviolent protest started in 1961. The "Freedom Rides" came about because, despite a Supreme Court ruling about integration on long-distance buses, many southern states simply ignored the law. Thirteen students, seven black and six white, decided to take the first Freedom Ride together, starting in Washington, D.C., and then heading south through the southern states to New Orleans, Louisiana.

The buses on which the students were traveling were attacked, and the students were badly beaten. The

◀ *Dr. King leaves an Atlanta shop in October 1960, under arrest for taking part in a lunch counter sit-in. Later that year presidential candidate John F. Kennedy intervened to have King released from jail.*

The Kennedys step in

In October 1960 Dr. King was arrested during a student sit-in in a store in Atlanta. He was put in jail with the students and held for many days. When the students were eventually released on bail, King was immediately rearrested on a technicality. He was transferred in chains to another jail and sentenced to four months' hard labor.

John F. Kennedy, who was running for president of the United States at that time, heard of King's situation. Both he and his brother, Senator Robert Kennedy, intervened on King's behalf. Dr. King was released, and thanked the Kennedys for their courage in helping him. In the election that followed in November, many African Americans voted for John F. Kennedy. He then became president of the United States.

second Freedom Ride ended in Montgomery. Dr. King traveled to the city to give the riders support. But as he was speaking to a mass meeting in Ralph Abernathy's church, a mob of white people surrounded the building. Stones and tear-gas bombs were thrown into the church and a car was set on fire.

The Freedom Rides continued, but in September 1961, new laws ended segregation on the buses for good.

▶ *This 1961 photo shows a bus set ablaze by anti-integration protesters during a "Freedom Ride."*

The Battle of Birmingham

In December 1961 Dr. King received a phone call from a young black man in Albany, Georgia. He asked King to go to Albany to speak at a mass meeting. Dr. King agreed.

The young man who phoned King was William G. Anderson, leader of a group of African-American protesters was were struggling against segregation in Albany. King had no intention of getting involved in their struggle, but he was happy to speak to the enthusiastic crowd he found at Shiloh Baptist Church. Yet when the leaders of the protest asked him to join their march the following day, such was the fervor of the people around him that he felt he could not refuse. It was the beginning of a long and bitter battle in Albany, which was only partially successful. King learned many lessons there.

Albany

On December 16, Dr. King led the protesters through the streets of Albany. The police were waiting for them, and arrested all the marchers and took them off to prison. King refused to pay his fine, electing to stay in prison instead. When negotiations started with the city authorities, King paid his bail and left prison, but it was soon obvious that the protest had done nothing to improve the situation in Albany.

In July of the following year, Dr. King was back in Albany. The SCLC decided to fight segregation on all fronts instead of targeting a particular service, for example, the buses. But the police had studied King's nonviolent protests and countered them with powerful tactics of their own. Time and time again, the protesters marched, were arrested, and were put into prison. The police used no

▶ *Albany, Georgia police chief Laurie Pritchett arrests Dr. King and other black protesters for praying on the front steps of Albany City Hall on July 27, 1962.*

violence, and consequently there was no brutality for newspaper journalists to report. Frustrated by the deadlock, violence eventually erupted in the black community, and there was a riot. King was distraught and called for a "Day of Penance" to show that he and his people were committed to peaceful protest without violence.

In a last attempt to keep the movement going in Albany, Dr. King and Ralph Abernathy led a small demonstration and were arrested once again. From July 27 to August 10, both men were held in jail, but to little effect. The protests weren't working and the city authorities still refused to negotiate about segregation. Regretfully, King left Albany and returned to Atlanta. The campaign in Albany had achieved little, but Dr. King learned from the mistakes made there. He decided to pursue the fight for desegregation in one of the most segregated cities in the South: Birmingham, Alabama.

Birmingham

According to Dr. King, Birmingham was "the most thoroughly segregated city in the country." Buses, schools, churches,

The lessons of Albany

In King's autobiography—an edited collection of his writings—he talks about some of the lessons learned from the experiences of Albany. He felt he had made a mistake in protesting against segregation generally, rather than one aspect of it, such as integrating the buses or lunch counters. He felt that generalizing had weakened the argument. King reflected that one small victory would have been symbolic, boosting morale and galvanizing support. Instead, people had left feeling depressed that nothing had been gained.

and even drinking fountains were all rigidly segregated. There was an atmosphere of fear and hatred in which white people who disliked the system were far too afraid to speak out, and in which African Americans were frequently attacked and sometimes killed. The city police commissioner, Eugene "Bull" Connor, was known for his racist views, and prided himself on his ability to keep black people "in their place."

▶ *Birmingham, Alabama police chief Eugene "Bull" Connor proved a difficult opponent, using fire hoses, dogs, and hundreds of police to quash civil rights protests.*

Before they started their campaign in Birmingham, Dr. King and the other SCLC leaders drew up a careful plan. It was called "Project C," the C standing for "Confrontation." The campaign started on April 3, 1963. The plan was to start modestly by targeting stores where the Jim Crow laws were enforced by staging sit-ins at their lunch counters. As predicted, the police arrested the protesters. Meanwhile, King held mass meetings every night in different churches, speaking about the campaign and explaining nonviolent resistance. At the end of each meeting, he would appeal for volunteers to join "Project C," and then ask them to give up any weapons they were carrying.

As the numbers of volunteers grew, the SCLC stepped up the demonstrations, and the jails began to fill up. One thing surprised the protesters: the police used virtually no violence as they rounded the demonstrators up. It seemed that "Bull" Connor was trying to copy the tactics of the police in Albany. All that was soon to change, however.

An act of faith

On April 10, the city obtained a court order to stop the protests. For the first time in his years of campaigning, Dr. King decided to break the law by ignoring the order. He knew that this would mean going back to prison, but he was ready to do so and to stay in for as long as necessary. Then another blow fell. The campaign needed funds to pay bail money for protesters in jail. If there was no money, the demonstrations would run out of volunteers because all the protesters would be stuck in prison. The city authorities had found a way to cut off the supply of money to the SCLC.

At a crisis meeting on April 12, Dr. King was told that if he went to jail, his campaign would have no money and the battle would be lost. The truth was that King was the only one with the contacts, and if he went back to prison the SCLC would not be able to continue.

It was one of the most difficult decisions of his whole life. After deep reflection, King replied that he didn't know what would happen or where the money would come from, but he must remain true to the cause.

Dr. King went straight from the meeting to the march. He was arrested and put into solitary confinement in prison. Alone in a dark cell, he began to

despair. Meanwhile Mrs. King, at home in Atlanta, was equally worried about her husband. She had not heard from him for two days. She decided to take some action and, remembering the kindness of the Kennedys (see page 47), she called President John F. Kennedy. The president called Birmingham and conditions

▲ *Water from a high-pressure fire hose slams into protesters as Birmingham police attempt to break up a 1963 demonstration.*

immediately improved for King. Better news followed. Thousands of dollars of bail money had been raised, and there was more if needed. Dr. King's faith had been rewarded.

The battle is won

Dr. King was released from prison after eight days. He decided to take another bold step to push the campaign. He asked for volunteers from schools and colleges to come forward. They too were trained in the ways of nonviolence, and on May 2, more than 1,000 young African Americans marched through Birmingham. The police arrested 900 of them. Another march followed the next day, this time with twice the number of young demonstrators. But "Bull" Connor had had enough. He ordered his men to turn fire hoses on the marchers, and then they let loose their dogs. The next morning, the nation's newspapers were filled with images of children and young people being knocked down and attacked by dogs.

The demonstrations continued, with more violence on the part of the police. Soon the city's jails were completely full. But business leaders in the city were beginning to weaken. They started negotiations with King and the other African-American leaders. The SCLC demanded desegregation in all stores in the city, better jobs for black people, the release of all protesters from jail, and a mixed-race group to plan for future desegregation. After a few days, the white leaders agreed to all the demands. The battle of Birmingham was won.

Aftermath

This was not the end of the story of Birmingham. The night after the agreement was made, there was a meeting of the Ku Klux Klan. Later on that night, the home of King's younger brother, Rev. A.D. King, was bombed, as was the motel in which Dr. King had stayed throughout the campaign. Luckily King was at home in Atlanta and his brother was not injured. Riots followed. Dr. King rushed back to Birmingham to try to calm the situation, and President Kennedy sent 3,000 troops to the city.

The city soon settled down, and King was able to look back with satisfaction on a successful campaign. He was sure that whatever happened from then on, the city of Birmingham would never be the same again.

◄ *Dr. King called off mass demonstrations in Birmingham on May 8, 1963, saying that honest attempts were being made to settle racial differences. He was later proved right.*

The March on Washington

For Dr. King the success of the Birmingham campaign was proof that nonviolent action was the right and only way forward. It also moved the president to propose a new, wide-ranging civil rights bill to Congress.

Throughout the summer of 1963, civil rights protests continued to grow, with marches, sit-ins, and picket lines across the country. The protestors' demands were simple: freedom and equality for African Americans everywhere. In the White House, President Kennedy decided that, at last, the time had come to ask Congress to pass a civil rights bill that would put an end to segregation. On the night of June 11, the president appeared on national television to talk about justice and civil rights. He would ask Congress to commit itself, he said, to the proposal "that race has no place in American life or law." Dr. King was delighted. Although the proposal was not as wide-ranging as he had hoped, it was a step in the right direction. Not everyone shared his views, however. The following night, Medgar Evers, a leader of the NAACP, was shot dead by a white man in front of his house in Jackson, Mississippi. This dreadful act revealed, King said, that, "we still have a long, long way to go in this nation before we achieve the ideals of decency and brotherhood."

Preparing to march

Meanwhile, two civil rights leaders, A. Philip Randolph and Bayard Rustin,

▶ The civil rights struggle goes to Washington. Dr. King poses at the White House with (from left to right) Rabbi Joachim Prinz, A. Philip Randolph, and President John F. Kennedy on August 29, 1963.

began to make plans for the now-famous March on Washington, D.C. King agreed to speak at the march, which Randolph and Rustin hoped would draw people from across the country and unite all the various voices of protest. The aims of the march were to demand jobs and freedom for African Americans and to urge Congress to pass the civil rights bill. The march was planned to end with a mass rally at the Lincoln Memorial.

The march leaders estimated that about 100,000 people would attend. But the actual number of marchers far exceeded their expectations. They were stunned by the size of the crowd. On the morning of August 28, 1963, at least 250,000 people from almost every state arrived in Washington, D.C. by bus, train, plane, and car. They were black and white, and included poor farmers from the deep South, teachers, ministers, and students, and even famous singers and movie stars.

◀ *Dr. King leads more than 250,000 people in the Freedom March on Washington on August 28, 1963.*

61

In the morning sun, they marched peacefully to the Lincoln Memorial, singing as they went.

"I have a dream"

At the Lincoln Memorial, the huge crowd spilled onto the lawns and began to listen to the speakers. Millions more people watched the rally on TV or listened on the radio. The final speaker was Martin Luther King Jr., the man everyone had come to hear. They would not be disappointed.

The speech King made on that day has become one of the most famous speeches of all time. He had prepared the text of his speech the night before and started off reading from it. But, seeing the huge crowd before him, King felt inspired. He abandoned his original speech and began to speak from the heart:

"I have a dream that one day this nation will rise up and live out the true meaning of its creed—we hold these truths to be self-evident; that all men are created equal.

"I have a dream that one day on the red hills of Georgia, the sons of former slaves and the sons of former slave owners will be able to sit down together at the table of brotherhood.

"I have a dream that one day even the state of Mississippi, a state sweltering with the heat of injustice, sweltering with the heat of oppression, will be transformed into an oasis of freedom and justice.

"I have a dream that my four little children will one day live in a nation where they will not be judged by the color of their skin but by the content of their character.

"I have a dream today!

"I have a dream that one day, down in Alabama, with its vicious racists, with its governor having his lips dripping with the words of interposition and nullification; one day right there in Alabama little black boys and black girls will be able to join hands with little white boys and girls as brothers and sisters.

"I have a dream today!

"I have a dream that one day every valley shall be exalted, every hill and mountain shall be made

▶ *King delivers his famous "I have a dream" speech at the Lincoln Memorial.*

low, the rough places will be made plain and the crooked places will be made straight and the glory of the Lord shall be revealed and all flesh shall see it together.

"This is our hope. This is the faith that I will go back to the South with. With this faith we will be able to hew out of the mountain of despair a stone of hope.

"With this faith we will be able to transform the jangling discords of our nation into a beautiful symphony of brotherhood. With this faith we will be able to work together, to pray together, to struggle together, to go to jail together, to stand up for freedom together, knowing that we will be free one day.

"This will be the day, this will be the day when all of God's children will be able to sing with new meaning: 'My country 'tis of thee, sweet land of liberty, of thee I sing. Land where my fathers died, land of the pilgrim's pride, from every mountainside, let freedom ring!'

▶ With the Washington Monument in the background, Dr. King acknowledges the crowd at the Lincoln Memorial.

And if America is to be a great nation, this must become true.

"And so let freedom ring from the prodigious hilltops of New Hampshire.

"Let freedom ring from the mighty mountains of New York.

"Let freedom ring from the heightening Alleghenies of Pennsylvania.

Malcolm X (1925–1965)

Not all black leaders supported Dr. King and his nonviolent tactics. Malcolm X was a leader of a religious group called the Black Muslims. At first, he did not believe in the integration of blacks and whites that Dr. King preached. He believed that black people had good reason to hate white people, and should be able to defend themselves, with violence if necessary. A year before he was assassinated, he changed some of his ideas and formed his own group, the Organization of Afro-American Unity, which was willing to work with anyone of any color to end injustice against African Americans.

◀ *In contrast to King's nonviolent approach, Black Muslim leader Malcolm X urged blacks to win their freedom "by any means necessary." He was assassinated in 1965.*

"Let freedom ring from the snow-capped Rockies of Colorado.

"Let freedom ring from the curvaceous slopes of California.

"But not only that.

"Let freedom ring from Stone Mountain of Georgia.

"Let freedom ring from Lookout Mountain of Tennessee.

"Let freedom ring from every hill and molehill of Mississippi, from every mountainside, let freedom ring!

"And when this happens, when we allow freedom to ring, when we let it ring from every village and every hamlet, from every state and every city, we will be able to speed up that day when all of God's children, black men and white men, Jews and Gentiles, Protestants and Catholics, will be able to join hands and sing in the words of the old Negro spiritual, 'Free at last, free at last. Thank God Almighty, we are free at last.'"

King's audience was spellbound. They cheered and shouted. Many were in tears. Nobody had any doubt: They had listened to history being made on that summer day in Washington, D.C.

Disaster and Triumph

After King's historic speech, the civil rights movement moved forward rapidly. But many shocking acts of violence were still carried out against African Americans.

On Sunday, September 15, 1963, just a few weeks after the triumphant Washington march, King was preaching at the Ebenezer Baptist Church when devastating news came from Birmingham, Alabama. A bomb had been thrown by a white segregationist into the Sixteenth Street Baptist Church, killing four young black girls and injuring 21 other children.

King hurried to the scene and was horrified by what he saw. As one woman said, "My God, we're not even safe in church!" A local member of the Ku Klux Klan was arrested, but the police eventually let him go (years later, in 1977, he was rearrested, tried for the bombing, and convicted of murder). After the successful "Battle for Birmingham" (see pages 50–57), this was a bitter blow for civil rights. At a funeral for three of the girls, King preached the eulogy. The girls did not die in vain, he said. They would be remembered as heroines who had died for the cause of freedom and dignity.

Kennedy assassinated

Two months later, on November 22, 1963, another appalling event rocked the entire country. On a visit to Dallas, Texas, President John F. Kennedy was shot dead by a sniper. Dr. King was at home in Atlanta, preparing for a fund-raising appearance, when he heard the news. Like the rest of America, he was shocked and stunned.

President Kennedy had not only been a great and dedicated president but, after a hesitant start, also a strong supporter of

▶ *President Kennedy rides with Mrs. Kennedy in an open car in Dallas, Texas, only moments before he was shot dead by a sniper on November 22, 1963.*

civil rights. Lee Harvey Oswald was arrested for Kennedy's murder. King, however, did not blame the president's death on the isolated act of a madman, but on a climate of hatred and violence.

Later, King wrote of Kennedy's death and how it had diminished everyone who had tolerated hatred, violence, and injustice. King mourned the man who had done so much for the civil rights movement in America and grieved because he felt that everyone, including himself, was culpable in his murder.

St. Augustine

By the end of 1963, some southern cities had made great strides toward freedom and equal rights for all their citizens. But in others segregation and racist violence remained a fact of life. In February 1964 Robert Hayling, a dentist and civil rights leader from the beautiful tourist town of St. Augustine, Florida, visited King in Atlanta and asked for his help.

St. Augustine was a stronghold of the Ku Klux Klan and other racist groups. Indeed, many of the town's deputies were prominent Klansmen. Its African-American population lived in constant fear of being beaten or killed by racist

thugs. Hayling's own house had been blasted with shotguns, almost killing his wife and two children. With no help forthcoming from Washington, the situation was becoming intolerable.

Dr. King readily agreed to help and vowed to make St. Augustine the next "nonviolent battlefield." He sent a small SCLC group ahead to mobilize the black community. They began to lead night marches to the old Slave Market in St. Augustine's public square, even though it was dangerous.

On the night of May 28, rioting broke out. While the police looked on, Klansmen attacked the marchers with iron pipes and bicycle chains. Hundreds of demonstrators were sent to jail and the night marches were banned.

King himself arrived in St. Augustine to take command and to raise people's spirits. Defying the ban on night marches, King and Abernathy marched to a local motel, where they were arrested and put in jail overnight. That night, a white mob attacked 400 black people, and tension

▶ *Dr. King and Ralph Abernathy pictured in St. John's County Jail on June 11, 1964. They were arrested while leading protests in St. Augustine. King described the jail as, "One of the nicest I've been in."*

continued to mount as white extremists whipped their supporters into a frenzy of antiblack feeling.

Events reached a peak on the night of June 25, when 800 Klansmen viciously attacked black marchers with clubs. King did not know what to do. His appeals to Washington to send in troops had fallen on deaf ears, and St. Augustine was turning into a nightmare. Luckily, the state governor realized how serious the situation had become and set up an emergency biracial committee to open up talks between the town's black and white leaders. It was what King had hoped for and he called the campaign off.

Civil Rights Act

Meanwhile, in Washington, the finishing touches were being put to the civil rights bill. After Kennedy's death, the new president, Lyndon B. Johnson, had asked Congress to pass the bill as soon as possible to honor Kennedy's memory. On July 2, 1964, King and other civil rights leaders were present in the White House as President Johnson signed the bill and and turned it into law.

The Civil Rights Act of 1964 banned racial discrimination in public places, such as hotels, restaurants, beaches, and parks, and called for equal opportunities in education and employment. The act still fell short on issues of voting rights, black poverty, and fair housing for everyone. So the fight would continue. Even so, it was a historic moment, and the act went a long way toward giving African Americans equal rights.

"Freedom Summer"

The summer of 1964 saw further campaigning in Mississippi. In the so-called "Freedom Summer," hundreds of civil rights workers set up freedom schools to teach African American adults how to register to vote. The white backlash soon began. In June, three young civil rights workers were murdered by white racists. State officials refused to allow them to be buried together, because one of them was black. A black woman, Fannie Lou Hamer, spoke on national television about the plight of black people in Mississippi. A former farm worker, she had been fired from her job and beaten up in jail for exercising her right to register to vote.

▶ *On July 2, 1964, President Lyndon Johnson signed the Civil Rights Bill, making it law, in a special ceremony in the East Room of the White House.*

Prize for peace

By now the name of Martin Luther King, Jr. was known and respected all over the world. King had been awarded many national and international prizes and distinctions. In October 1964, while he was taking a well-earned rest, the news came that he had won the Nobel Prize for Peace, the highest honor of all. King was delighted but he remained very humble about his achievement. He later wrote that the prize was not his alone. It had been won by all of his people, who had shown great wisdom, courage, and restraint throughout a long campaign for justice and respect. They had taken a nonviolent course to bring about "a rule of love across this nation of ours."

In December, King flew to Oslo to receive his prize from the King of Norway. In his acceptance speech, he painted a vivid picture of the civil rights struggle. Dr. King stated that he was mindful of the fact that only recently civil rights protesters in the southern United States had been attacked with fire hoses and

◀ *A photograph taken on December 12, 1964 of Dr. King holding the Nobel Peace Prize Gold Medal. King donated the prize money, $54,600, to the SCLC and other civil rights groups.*

The Nobel Prizes

The Nobel Prizes were established by Swedish chemist and inventor of dynamite, Alfred Nobel (1833–1896). By nature, Nobel was a pacifist, and he worried about the potential misuse of the explosives he had invented. He set up a fund to provide annual awards for outstanding achievement in the fields of science, literature, and international peace (an economics prize was added later). The awards were first given in 1901. At age 35, Martin Luther King, Jr. was the youngest winner in Nobel history, and the third black person to win the Nobel Prize for Peace.

dogs and that others had been beaten and killed. He spoke of the grinding poverty that affected African Americans, locking them into despair. He accepted the Nobel Prize on behalf of the entire civil rights movement as an affirmation that nonviolence was the only answer to the world's most crucial political and moral questions.

King concluded his inspiring words by saying that he accepted the award with an audacious faith in mankind and adding that he "... refused to accept despair as the final response to the ambiguities of history."

Voting Rights

Although every citizen in the United States, black and white, had the right to vote, many blacks were denied that right. Now King turned his attention to pushing forward a voting-rights bill.

Passed in 1870, the 15th amendment of the U.S. constitution states: "The right of citizens of the United States to vote shall not be denied or abridged by the United States or by any state on account of race, color, or previous condition of servitude [slavery]." But, almost 100 years later, most black people in the southern states were still denied the right to vote.

In order to vote, they first had to register, and many measures were used to prevent this, such as so-called literacy tests, which were too difficult for anyone to pass, and special taxes, which poor black people could not afford to pay.

Since 1957 King and the civil rights movement had worked hard to expose the injustices of the system and to register black people to vote (see page 42). Now they took the fight for justice to the town of Selma, Alabama.

Project Alabama

The campaign planned for Selma was nicknamed "Project Alabama." In Selma, more than half the population of 29,000 were black, yet black people only accounted for one voter in every 100. Here, schools were segregated and black people were expected "to know their place" as inferior to whites. Almost any measure was used to keep black people from voting, including asking them to recite a long state law from memory to be allowed to register. The Board of Registrars rejected black applications for the most minor reasons, such as failing to cross a letter "t" on the registration form.

King hoped that nonviolent protest marches and demonstrations would bring about changes in the system, as they had in Birmingham. But he had a powerful enemy in the town's sheriff, Jim Clark, a tough segregationist and racist. Clark vowed to "preserve the white way of life and not let black people take over the state."

▲ King, Abernathy, and other demonstrators face Selma Sheriff Jim Clark in 1965 as Clark orders them to disperse.

King later said: "I knew that if I looked Clark in the eye he would have hit me."

Courthouse under siege

In early January 1965, Dr. King and Ralph Abernathy arrived in Selma. They drove along Highway 80, which linked Selma to Montgomery, the state capital. King's first stop was a local church, where he told the waiting people that this day marked the start of a well-organized campaign to secure the right to vote in Alabama. He went on to say that their cry was a simple one: "Give us the ballot!"

On January 18, King was back in Selma for the first march of the campaign in which he led 400 African Americans to the courthouse to register. The marchers were met by Sheriff Clark, who turned them away.

Naming a successor

During Project Alabama, Dr. King received a large number of threats against his life. At a meeting of the SCLC, King told his friends that if he died, Ralph Abernathy was to succeed him as president of the movement. Abernathy was reluctant to become King's successor, stating that he did not look forward to filling the shoes of Martin Luther King, Jr. He believed that no one could take King's place.

Over the next few weeks the marches continued. Thousands of people were arrested and sent to jail, including King and Abernathy. From his cell, King kept busy, sending instructions to his followers about how Project Alabama should proceed. Shortly afterward, King was released on bail.

The march to Montgomery

On the night of February 18, 1965, a young black marcher, Jimmie Lee Jackson, was shot by police during a peaceful demonstration in Marion, a nearby town. He was rushed to a hospital in Selma, where Dr. King visited him. A few days later, Jackson died. After his funeral, King announced that he was stepping up the campaign. On Sunday, March 7, there would be a mass protest march from Selma to Montgomery. King was in fighting mood. With rousing words he told his people that they must stand up for what was right, even though there might be violent retaliation against them.

▶ *Dr. King leaves jail after nearly a week behind bars on February 5, 1965. To the right is Selma Public Safety Director, Wilson Baker, ordering reporters to leave.*

The governor of Alabama, George Wallace, banned the march and told the police to use whatever means were available to make sure the marchers were stopped. But the marchers were not put off. On Sunday morning, more than 500 people began to march to Montgomery. They did not get far. Just outside the town, they were met by a wall of state troopers, standing three deep across Highway 80, wearing gas masks and armed with clubs. As the marchers approached, a trooper ordered them to turn around. They had two minutes to do as he said. The marchers refused to move and the troopers attacked, brutally beating them back with their clubs before firing tear gas at them. A group of Sheriff Clark's men joined in the attack, on horseback, lashing the marchers with whips. Reeling from the blows, the marchers retreated. More than 140 people were injured during the violence.

The ministers' march

News of the bloody attack was broadcast on television news and printed in the newspapers. The American public was shocked at what they saw. Back in Atlanta, King was horrified. He felt guilty that he had not been there to share the marchers' ordeal. He ordered another march for Tuesday, March 9. At King's request, some 400 religious leaders rushed to Selma, including ministers, priests, and rabbis, black and white, to join him and hundreds of other marchers in the so-called "ministers' march." Because of recent threats on his life, King's friends were very worried about his safety. But he insisted that nobody would stop him from going to Selma and marching as planned. "We've gone too far to turn back now," he told a meeting of fellow protesters. "We must let them know that nothing can stop us, not even death itself." This time, faced with the state troopers, the marchers knelt and prayed, then turned back of their own accord.

That night three white ministers that supported the civil rights movement were attacked by a gang of white racists in Selma. One of them, Rev. James Reeb from Boston, was beaten in the head with a club, and died two days later. His murder caused outrage across the country. In the White House, President Johnson called it, "an American tragedy which cannot and

will not be repeated," and vowed to push a new voting rights bill forward. In a television address, the president told the country: "It is wrong, deadly wrong, to deny any of your fellow Americans the right to vote. Their cause must be our cause, too. Because it's not just black people, but really it's all of us who must overcome the crippling legacy of bigotry and injustice." As King had hoped, events in Selma had shown people what was really going on, even though it had taken the death of a white minister to convince them that something needed to be done.

▲ *Alabama state troopers fire tear gas and arrest civil rights protesters at Selma on March 7, 1965. Their brutality shocked Americans from coast to coast.*

Montgomery at last

Two days after the president's address, Judge Johnson ordered Governor Wallace to allow the Selma-to-Montgomery march to take place and to give the marchers police protection. President Johnson dispatched hundreds of Alabama National Guardsmen and U.S. military police to do this job. Wallace was furious, but King and his followers were overjoyed. On the morning of Sunday, March 21, more than 3,000 people gathered in Selma, ready to march. King told them that despite the poverty and inequality they had endured for so long and on such a grand scale, they still had physical strength to march and an unwearying spirit to endure the fight.

With King and Abernathy at their front, the marchers set out along Highway 80, on their way to Montgomery. Several hundred white people lined the roadside, heckling them as they passed. At night, some of the marchers headed back to Selma, by bus and car. Others slept in tents, guarded by state troopers. The next morning, they set out again. As they walked, the marchers chanted:

"Old Wallace, never can jail us all.
Old Wallace, segregation's bound to fall.
Pick 'em up and put 'em down
All the way to Montgom'ry town."

The march to Montgomery took five days. By the time they reached the city, the marchers were weary but jubilant. Thousands more protestors, black and white, came to join them.

▶ Journey's end: Thousands of marchers arrive in Montgomery, led by Dr. and Mrs. King.

On Thursday, March 25, King led 25,000 people through the streets of Montgomery, up Dexter Avenue, where his old church still stood, to the white building of the Alabama State Capitol to petition Governor Wallace for black voting rights. The marchers could see the governor peeking out of the window, but he refused to come out and talk to them. In the full glare of television cameras, King then gave one of his most stirring speeches, saying that the civil rights movement in Alabama was now unstoppable and that there was no going back.

The right to vote

In the end, Project Alabama proved a great success, despite the brutality and violence. Events in Selma and Montgomery were reported all over America. News of Dr. King's imprisonment made national headlines, and the state troopers' bloody attack on the marchers was broadcast nationwide. Pressure mounted on the local white authorities to make it easier for black people to register to vote. In the White House, President Johnson could not ignore King's wishes for much longer.

The Voting Rights Act

The 1965 Voting Rights Act made it illegal for the southern states to prevent African Americans from registering to vote. It banned literacy tests and other requirements. From then on, elections in the South would be closely monitored to ensure that as many people as possible registered to vote. The law had a huge effect. Over the next three years, in Alabama alone, the number of registered African Americans rose by 150 percent. In 1982 U.S. president Ronald Reagan tried to withdraw the law on the grounds that it was no longer needed. In protest, civil rights groups marched again from Selma to Montgomery. The law was allowed to stand.

He asked Congress to pass a new voting rights bill. In August the bill became the Voting Rights Act of 1965. King flew to Washington for the official signing. For Dr. King and the marchers of Selma, Alabama, it was a truly historic victory.

▶ *President Johnson presented Dr. King with the pen he used to sign the Voting Rights Act into law. It became one of King's most treasured possessions.*

Poverty and Peace

For many people, Project Alabama was Martin Luther King Jr.'s finest hour. Now he turned his attention away from the South to the cities of the North.

In the summer of 1964, rioting had broken out in the poor, overcrowded black neighborhoods of several northern cities. The following summer, King flew to Puerto Rico to attend a religious conference and to have a well-earned rest. While he was gone, the Watts area of Los Angeles erupted in the worst race riots ever seen. For six days, black rioters burned and looted shops and stores before the police could stop them. Thirty-four people were killed, and hundreds more injured. Thousands were arrested, and millions of dollars worth of damage was done. It was a major setback to the civil rights movement. King was horrified.

He flew to Los Angeles to visit the scene of the riot, pleading with people to adopt nonviolent ways. But the people he met were in no mood to talk about nonviolence. They were frustrated and angry with their lot.

Some even heckled him. But Dr. King understood why.

A meeting in Watts

Although King hated violence, he understood the reasons why people felt they had no other choice but to riot. To illustrate this, he recounted a meeting in Watts during the riots. A young man had said to King afterwards: "We won." When King pointed out that more than 30 people had died in the rioting and how could he say it was a victory, the youth replied: "We made them pay attention to us."

King believed that when people feel they have no voice they often resort to temper tantrums to get attention, in the way that a child would. He thought that riots were like huge temper tantrums thrown by neglected, frustrated people.

▶ *Martin Luther King Jr.'s forceful speaking style is captured in this photo of his address to a rally in Philadelphia on August 4, 1965.*

Causes of riots

The reasons for the riots were glaringly obvious to King. Despite the successes of the civil rights movement, many African Americans felt that they had suffered for a long time and that nobody seemed to care. They rioted because they were angry and desperate.

In the cities, most black people were very poor and many had poor-paying jobs or no jobs at all. They lived in overcrowded, congested neighborhoods where greedy landlords charged them huge rents for houses that were damp, rundown, and infested with rats and cockroaches. Unless something was done for them, violence would never be far from the surface. In his previous campaigns, King had concentrated on the problems of segregation and voter registration. Now he turned his attention to the poverty, unemployment, and slum conditions endured by many blacks.

Chicago campaign

Dr. King chose the northern city of Chicago, Illinois, for his first major civil rights campaign in the North. In January 1966 he announced the start of the "Chicago Campaign" to demand better living conditions for the city's black people. The thrust of the nonviolent campaign was to protest against the "violence of poverty" as well as the "violence of segregation."

King himself moved into an apartment in a poor black neighborhood, known as "Slumdale," where he planned to stay during the campaign. The apartment was cramped, dingy, and bitterly cold and cost more than a bigger, modern apartment in a white neighborhood.

In the months that followed, King toured the black neighborhoods of Chicago, giving talks and speeches, and urging people to join him in his nonviolent campaign. He even visited the leaders of Chicago's violent youth gangs, asking them to give nonviolent protest a chance. More than 200 gang members agreed to follow King's example. On July 10, so-called "Freedom Sunday," 30,000 people gathered in the sweltering heat at Soldier Field to hear King give a speech that marked the real

▶ This photograph of a poor neighborhood in 1960s Chicago. It was people living in these kinds of conditions that King wished to help.

launch of the campaign. Then King led them in a march to City Hall with a set of demands for the mayor. They included demands to end unfair housing and police brutality against blacks, and to create more jobs.

In front of the cheering crowd, King stuck the list of demands on the door of City Hall. The next day, he returned to present them to Mayor Richard J. Daley. If Daley did not act, King said, the streets of Chicago would be taken over by sit-ins, boycotts, and demonstrations.

On July 12, however, disaster struck. Rioting broke out on Chicago's West Side, triggered by the summer weather. To cope with the baking heat, youths had turned on the fire hydrants in the streets to keep cool. As the police tried to turn the hydrants off, fighting broke out, and hundreds of angry black youths took to the streets, breaking windows and pelting police cars with rocks. King appealed for calm, but it was no use. The riots continued.

By the morning of July 15, two people were dead, many more were injured, and hundreds were in jail. Thousands of soldiers were dispatched to the West Side to restore law and order. King also met the gang leaders and asked them to put a stop to the violence.

More marches

In August 1966 Dr. King announced another series of marches to appeal against segregated housing and slum conditions. On August 5, he led 600 marchers, black and white, escorted by 900 police through an all-white neighborhood. As the marchers gathered in Marquette Park, a crowd of angry white onlookers pelted them with bottles, bricks, rocks, and other projectiles. One brick hit King on the head. But he insisted that the march should proceed as planned.

As the marchers passed, the crowd shouted racist remarks and continued to throw things at them. In the chaos, a knife was thrown at King. It missed him and hit a white youth in the shoulder. Somehow the marchers reached Marquette Park again safely, but the march set off such scenes of hatred against black people that many white people were stunned.

▶ *Fellow marchers force Dr. King down for his own safety after he was struck with a brick during a march in Chicago in August 1966.*

King did not give up. Although he was tired of marching, he said he would not stop until African Americans had justice. Over the next week, more marches occured, stirring up more hatred and violence.

Finally, Mayor Daley decided that the time had come to take notice of what King was saying. On August 26, he agreed to meet King at City Hall to try to work something out. For King, this was a tremendous breakthrough. For the first time, the mayor was admitting the problems facing the city's black people. In the so-called "Summit Agreement," reached at the meeting, it was agreed that fair housing, better jobs, and equal rights and opportunities must now be the city's top priorities.

Speaking out

Many civil rights leaders criticized the Chicago Campaign and said that it had achieved very little. King was also criticized for speaking out against the Vietnam War.

By 1966 the United States was getting deeper and deeper into the war that had already been raging for five years. Thousands of Americans had already died and many people wanted to see an end to U.S. involvement. But President Johnson continued to send troops and war planes to Vietnam, and millions of Americans supported his actions. King objected to war because he hated violence. Furthermore, he did not think that the United States should meddle in another country's affairs.

Despite advice against it, and to the president's fury, he vowed to continue to speak out against the war.

The Vietnam War (1961–1975)

In 1954 an international agreement divided the southeast Asian country of Vietnam into communist North Vietnam and noncommunist South Vietnam. Pro-communist Viet Cong rebels in the south, helped by North Vietnam, soon began to fight for a unified, communist state. Worried about the spread of communism in the region, the United States backed South Vietnam and sent in its first troops in 1961. Despite a huge U.S. presence, the Viet Cong won victory after victory. By the end of 1973, realizing the war could not be won, the United States withdrew. Fighting continued until 1975, when South Vietnam was brought under North Vietnamese control.

▲ *Antiwar protesters march to the United Nations in New York on April 15, 1967. King spoke out against increasing U.S. involvement in Vietnam.*

King may have hoped that his antiwar protests would help to mend the growing rifts in the civil rights movement. King had already begun to lose the support of many young people who thought that nonviolence was not working and wanted to see more violent approaches to the civil rights struggle. Among his fiercest critics were the SNCC (Student Nonviolent Coordinating Committee), who wanted to be able to fight back if they were attacked. King was horrified to see the SNCC leaders traveling across the country, stirring up the crowds with their "Black Power" war cry. He was afraid that it would push blacks and whites farther apart, instead of bringing greater understanding. For him, nonviolence was still the only answer.

Free at Last

At the beginning of 1968, poverty was still very much on King's mind. He was soon busy planning a "Poor People's Campaign" to take place in Washington, D.C., in late April

In March, before heading for Washington, King went to Memphis, Tennessee. The city's sanitation workers, almost all of them black, were demanding better wages and working conditions as well as recognition of their trade union. When the authorities refused to address their complaints, they went on strike. Their leaders asked King to come to Memphis to give speeches and support the strike. For King these were exactly the people he was hoping his Poor People's Campaign would help, and he readily agreed to go.

In Memphis thousands of people came to hear him speak. King called for black workers to boycott their jobs and for children to stay away from school to join him on a huge nonviolent march.

The march was planned for Friday, March 22, but had to be rescheduled for March 28, because of heavy snowfall. Soon after the marchers started, trouble began. Some black teenagers started smashing windows and looting stores in the name of Black Power. King called the march off. "I will never lead a violent march," he said.

The rioting and violence that followed the march greatly saddened King. He even thought about stepping aside and letting others lead the movement. But he could not do so. He vowed to come back to Memphis and lead another march, to prove to his doubters that nonviolence could still succeed.

The mountaintop

On April 3, Dr. King boarded a flight for Memphis, to attend the next march planned for Friday, April 5. On this occasion the flight was delayed by a

▶ *Dr. and Mrs. King are pictured in the mid-1960s with three of their children: Yolanda (on arm of chair), Martin Luther III (standing at left), and Dexter Scott.*

bomb threat. The pilot explained that because Dr. Martin Luther King, Jr. was on board, the plane and all the bags had to be checked thoroughly. Indeed, the plane had been guarded all night. King, who had received many threats over the years, shrugged off this incident.

In Memphis King and Abernathy checked into the Lorraine Motel. That evening, Dr. King addressed a crowd of about 2,000 people at the Bishop Mason Temple. In a stirring speech, he talked about the struggle ahead. He recalled being stabbed in New York, and the bomb threat that morning. King stated that he would like to live a long time, but that if his life were cut short for any reason that it would be the will of God. It was the last speech he ever made.

Assassination

The next morning King met with his colleagues in his motel room to discuss the forthcoming march. After lunch, he spent time with his brother who was also staying there. That evening, King and his staff had been invited out to dinner at a local clergyman's house. King changed his clothes, then went to stand on the balcony while he waited for the others. It was a chilly evening and Solomon Jones, King's devoted driver, tried to persuade him to put on a warm coat. King was touched by Solomon's concern and asked Abernathy if he would get his coat.

Suddenly, there was a rifle shot. A bullet smashed into King's face, knocking him backward. Then he fell to the ground. Martin Luther King, Jr. died in a hospital about one hour later.

It was April 4, 1968. Dr. King was 39 years old.

"Free at last"

King's murder produced shock, anger, and grief across the country and abroad. Rioting broke out in more than a hundred U.S. cities. President Johnson declared Sunday, April 7, as a national day of mourning. Meanwhile, the hunt was on for King's assassin, who had been seen speeding away from the crime. He was named as James Earl Ray, an escaped white convict. At his trial, Ray pleaded guilty to killing King and was sentenced to 99 years in jail. He later tried to withdraw his plea, but his conviction stood.

▶ *King and Abernathy pictured on the balcony of the Lorraine Motel, Memphis, Tennessee on April 4, 1968. With them is the civil rights leader Jesse Jackson (left).*

King's body was flown home to Atlanta, Georgia, to lie in state. Thousands of weeping mourners filed past to pay their last respects. On April 9, 1968 King's funeral took place at Ebenezer Baptist Church, where he had been pastor with his father. The church was packed and thousands more people stood outside, listening to the service over loudspeakers.

Afterward, Dr. King's coffin was placed on a farm cart pulled by two mules, a symbol of his Poor People's Campaign. Then, with some 50,000 people marching behind, and millions more watching on television, King's body was taken to South View Cemetery, where he was buried near his grandparents. On his gravestone were carved the words of the old African-American spiritual, which he had quoted so many times:

"Free at last, free at last.

Thank God Almighty, I'm free at last."

◄ *This police reconstruction shows the view that Dr. King's killer must have had through his telescopic sight as he aimed at the Lorraine Motel balcony where King was standing on April 4, 1968.*

Martin Luther King, Jr.'s Legacy

Martin Luther King, Jr.'s assassination sent shock waves around the world. But his work did not end with his death. The civil rights movement lived on, trying to achieve justice and equality for everyone regardless of color or race.

By the time of his death, Dr. King had already helped to change American society. Many cities had been forced to abandon laws that discriminated against black people and to pass laws that made segregation illegal. Black voters were now able to exercise their right to vote.

King had also tried to show people that violence was not the way to get things changed. Nonviolence was a much more powerful weapon. After his death, the civil rights movement continued. King himself said that, if he had never been born, there would have been a civil rights movement. There comes a time, he said, when injustice must end.

Today in the United States, African Americans have achieved equality under the law, but there is still a long way to go. White people still tend to have better-paying jobs, more opportunities, and live in better neighborboods than black people. And there are still many people who are racially prejudiced. However, many black people have achieved high office; in the 1980s Jesse Jackson, a close colleague of King's, ran for president.

▶ *Martin Luther King, Jr.'s funeral took place on April 9, 1968. His coffin was carried on a farm cart drawn by two mules. This photo shows the procession just after leaving Ebenezer Baptist Church.*